To Joan
with appreciation for love
of good poetry.
Paul B. Fleeth
October 1944

COAL

– Taxus Press –

*For John Tomkins, coal-miner,
died of silicosis, December 14th 1975*

COAL

John Gurney
and
Paul Peter Piech

COAL
First edition 1994
Poems © John Gurney
Art © Paul Peter Piech
All rights reserved

ISBN 1 873012 68 3

ACKNOWLEDGEMENTS
The exhibition 'Coal' has appeared at
The Old Library, Cardiff; The Glyn Vivian Gallery, The
Ceri Richards Gallery, The Taliesin Gallery, Swansea;
The Dua Park Gallery, Aberdeen.
Poems & graphics have appeared in
*The London Magazine, Acumen, Orbis, Barn, Tribune
The New Welsh Review, The New Statesman and Society*
and *Westwords.*

Published by
TAXUS PRESS
at Stride
11 Sylvan Road
Exeter
Devon
EX4 6EW
England

Contents

Introduction *7*

Incrimination *10*
Headstocks *12*
The Collier's Dawn *14*
Miners' Photograph *16*
Slavery *18*
Riding The Shaft *20*
Remembering Mine Children *22*
The Infernal Machine *24*
Beauty *26*
The Lamp-House *28*
Thin Seams *30*
Postures *32*
Chocks *34*
The Viewer *36*
The Fireman *38*
The Timekeeper *40*
The Ventilator *42*
Overmen *44*
The Collier *46*
Accidents *48*
The Fire *50*
Sculptures *52*
Corpses *54*
The Lamp *56*
Methane *58*
Waters *60*
Lovers *62*
Magic *64*
The Pit Stack *66*
Suffering *68*

Tarts *70*
Revenants *72*
Zion Chapel *74*
The Farrier *76*
Blind Horses *78*
Pit Horses *80*
Holidays *82*
Explosions *84*
Coal Trains *86*
Mourning, Morning *88*
Nature *90*
The Coal Picker *92*
Washerwomen *94*
Fighting Wives *96*
Pit Village *98*
The Resurrection *100*
The Flood (I) *102*
Snow *104*
The Magic Apple Tree *106*
Strike *108*
Dole Queue *110*
Coal Pickers *112*
The Engine Man's Dream *114*
The Driver *116*
Mars *118*
Silicosis *120*
In The Water *122*
The Survivor *124*
Ghosts *126*
The Derelict Engine House *128*
Closure *130*
History *132*

"ANGER IS NOT ENOUGH"

"Anger is not enough..." These were the words of Michael McGahey, then Vice President of the National Union of Mine Workers, at a conference after the miners were industrially defeated in 1984/1985. His message was that if anger were enough then our parents and grandparents could have sorted out all our problems. In that most powerful speech, full of his own anger, and also the pathos of decades of struggles and set-backs, there was also something else. That something else is conveyed in the images of Paul Peter Piech and the words of John Gurney.

Their images and words are certainly full of anger and pathos. But, as with the visionary words and images of Michael McGahey, there is also a sense of solidarity. Michael McGahey had learnt through struggle that there was a need for action to be guided by thought. And in the work of Paul Pieter Piech and John Gurney there is that fine sense of solidarity born out of collective action and thought with the subject, rather than a distanced sympathy. That solidarity is about the way in which the artist identifies with the subject whether it be the miners at their work, the women of our valley communities, or the horses which laboured for generations underground.

There is undoubtedly something quite evocative and nostalgic in all this work. But there is also an imperceptible and immeasurable sense of purpose and solidarity about these words and images. There is no romance or paternalistic sympathy for the downtrodden. The starkness prevents all of that. Nevertheless there is something new and different about the combination of words and images provided by these artists. They tell a story of an age and time that has gone, or so it seems, but it is an age and time which still invades the present: ever since last Autumn wider "society" has recognised – albeit a little too late – the value and worth of miners and their communites past and present, even though we hardly have a coalfield left in Wales or elsewhere.

More than that, what is also conveyed is that communities are made up of individual human beings whose suffering is very often lonely and isolated. I well recall the late Dick Beamish of Abercrave contrasting the justifiable publicity for a mining disaster of the magnitude of Senghenydd or Aberfan with the loneliness of the death of a pneumoconiotic miner at home surrounded by only his immediate family. The scale of suffering to the human being – man or woman – is as harrowing for one family as it is for a hundred.

On the lighter side, thankfully, there are happy times in valley communities. We do get a sense of neighbourliness, community and solidarity in these images. Paul Peter Piech and John Gurney in their different ways bring out the best of our collectivist culture. I particularly like the evocative images provided by 'the coal pickers' and 'the timbermen', who through their collective 'art' create their own beauty.

But my favourite image is that of the spirit of the horse 'on holidays'. I well recall as a child the horses from Banwen during the miners' fortnight enthusiastically rushing – indeed galloping, down Wembley Avenue – to the open fields of Seven Sisters in mid Summer, and by contrast their lack of enthusiasm on their return to another fifty weeks of what A. J. Cook, in another age called "the dark dungeons of despair". In those days it was part of our way of life, but one does wonder in this day and age whether such inhumanity would ever be accepted. It was in a time when the 'condemning' of men to darkness, and women to support them in the drudgery and hardship of their unpaid domestic work, was something that was accepted and so too was the denying of sunlight to horses for most of their lives.

Doubtless these words and images would convey different things to different people, depending on their memories and their received memories. For me, the last thought should be with those who experienced much of what is beautifully conveyed by John Gurney and Paul Peter Piech. My great grandfather was taken to work in the 1860's as a seven year old boy in the Swansea Valley, in order that his father could claim extra trams to fill. That story was told to me by my father, who explained that the boy was led to one side to sleep whilst his father laboured to fill the extra trams. 'Mine children', therefore, has a particular memory, albeit a received one for me. Many might say that those days are gone and thankfully gone. But so long as men, women, and children (in other parts of the world women and children still do so) risk their lives to hew the coal then we must be constantly aware of the dangers that they face in order to bring light and heat to our "civilised" world. For that reason alone the images and words of Paul Peter Piech and John Gurney provide a service to us all, particularly in South Wales, because they remind us of our collective inheritance.

Hywell Francis
24 August 1993

Hywel Francis is the co-author of *The Fed: A History of the South Wales Miners in the Twentieth Century* and *Miners Against Fascism*. He is also one of the founders of the South Wales Miners' Library.

INCRIMINATION

Half-paralysed by guilt, amorphous pain,
I trespass as an alien in a land
I have no right to enter. Once again
lost life begins to flicker through my hand
as I begin to wander through this mine
in the dyed light, plot to save or kill
in the black deeps. Now consciousness defines
a headstocks and a cage, begins to thrill
with new incriminations, confident
that all will sound quite bogus. Now I feel
quite sure of condemnation, punishment,
and overwhelmed by joy that I must kneel,
do penance to the land, as what I've dreamed
appears to work salvation, things redeemed.

HEADSTOCKS

Headstocks, built of pitchpine or of steel,
intrigue the eye. Their canted lattice-work
soon draws it in, like bridges. Their pulley-wheels
will swiftly wind attention through the murk
of pitheads. Co-ordinated, turning
in their opposite directions, two
shafts working on one rope. Quickly circling
through the smoke, the dirty wind. Lifting shoes
on rails. Tall, hieratic gantries, stronger
far since catches were invented, safety hooks
preventing overwinding, the lander's
nightmare. One has read in many books
of accidents where men, despite their hymns,
were hurled across a wheel towards a whim.

THE COLLIER'S DAWN

Gradually his will grew paralysed.
Waking, stiff with dread before the dawn,
he lay alone, inert, devitalised
as slag-banks. Cursed, dragged out of bed, sworn
into activity, he'd stumble round
the scullery, each simple ritual act
a dragging, black aversion. Underground,
a pit smoked. It waited to exact
an adequate revenge. A belt wrecked.
A spanner thrust into an engine. Gas
fired. An old dam holed. Something to correct
the balance of existence, the morass
of slurry in some saturated drift,
the angling for a wet-note every shift.

MINERS' PHOTOGRAPH

Despite the sunlight slanting on their eyes
the background's black. A miners' photograph.
Flat caps set like berets. No sign of ties,
just mufflers, with no collars. No one laughs
towards us, though a young man starts to lift
an eyebrow. There's a casual cigarette
stuck sideways in his mouth. Behind, the shaft.
The ordeal of the cage. A dark vignette.
Their clothes are clean, their faces. Safety lamps
are dangling from their hands. Polished, bright,
some stand up in the slack. Soon they'll be cramped
up, birthwise. That man there on the right
could swear for seven minutes, constantly,
without one repetition. Violently.

SLAVERY

Simone Weil said it. Slavery is work
without eternal light or poetry,
without religion. Such knowledge irks.
The spirit feels disgust. One could see
it in the cage. Ascending was pure joy.
Men sprinted from the shaft into the showers.
Descending was quite different. Destroyed
the soul. Men would contemplate the hours
before them at the coal-face. Would prefer
the second cage. Went silent as they'd make
the long trip down the road. Would not confer.
Just sat there, three a bench, just half-awake,
knees interlocked. At length they would uncoil.
Disperse to separate areas of toil.

RIDING THE SHAFT

Formerly, of course, they had no cage.
Instead they used a rope and knotted chain
that held three hooks. Men would disengage
the baskets, fixed the links back. Were constrained,
two at a time, to slip one leg and knee
through the thick noose. They held on with one arm,
the other grasped a lad precariously
who gripped like iron. And then, to some alarm,
the shackles dropped. The other lengths would fill,
all space be taken up by clinging boys,
like long-lined fish. And women's bodies, shrill,
would oscillate through shaft-smoke, and enjoy
the burnings, as hot limbs would intermesh
a thick, descending pendulum of flesh.

REMEMBERING MINE CHILDREN

At times they would return, like images
of a deprived childhood. Utilitarian
children. Bleeding, blackened, like savages,
girded round the waist, a heavy chain
beneath their legs, hitched up to the trams
by dog-belts, hempen harnesses, a guss.
Stark naked boys, who worked their diagrams
of darkness. She could see them, luminous,
in the dark pit. Girls stripped down to their thighs,
their skulls scalped by the roof. Their bodies gassed
by blackdamp. Their small knees damaged by
the dropped coal in the tunnels as they passed
from face to road. Their hips half-crippled, brains
impacted in their stationary pain.

THE INFERNAL MACHINE

You see its shape, the strange mechanics
of its angles, winding ropes, the whim?
It's difficult at dusk. Light plays odd tricks
with vision. You're getting it? The grim
precision of the cage, the downcast shaft?
The Dukie engine, then the spinning fan
that drags gas from the levels? Feel the draught?
That roar of sheer afflictiion? It trepans.
A mine, of course. Like Kafka's strange machine
for torture. One that will inscribe a
judgement in the flesh. That will define
a time to kill you. Victims always die, the
smile of pure redemption on a face
whose guilt has been remitted, full of grace.

BEAUTY

Beauty's the experimental proof
of incarnation. Is in everything
that gives authentic wonder. Under roofs
of coal, even transport lads were suffering
from glory, thumbing through pornography
by cap-lamp light. The idle engineers
would worship women's bodies through the see
of rollers and conveyors, with their ears
deaf to the shearers. Even they perhaps
experienced the facts of paradise
a little, of externals that collapse
in splendour as the thresh of legs and thighs
proclaims, as human flesh is stretched and rolled,
the body is in fact inside the soul.

THE LAMP-HOUSE

The night would be as black as anthracite
as men filed past the window, calling out
their numbers. The lamp-man then would light
their lantern, check on its condition, shout
his comments. The safety-lamp, in pits,
was a mixed blessing. Owners, craftily,
at once expected men to work with it
in places filled with gas, where formerly
they could not toil by candles. The lamps
were checked, too, at the bottom for the smear
of coal-dust grease. It could well fire the damps.
Anyone who tried to interfere
with them was sacked. They knew the colliers' games.
Some men took off the gauze for better flames.

THIN SEAMS

Some seams were thin. Just eighteen inches thick.
A little low for comfort. None the less
much higher than one thought. One learnt the trick
of coping. Half an inch reduced the stress.
One soon became accustomed, soon would find
it easier to shift the broken coal
when lying down, relaxing when reclined.
Some seams were far too narrow to control
a filler's shovel. It had been known for men
to crawl for fifty yards along the face
to turn a blade so it was once again
the right way up, to squirm back through the place
right to the mulligate. They then would claw
a path back in-between the roof and floor.

POSTURES

Postures of men who mined the coal
depended on the height at which they'd work.
In some seams they could stand, but on the whole
most started on their knees, bent up in murk
like Atlas, or some strangely praying priest.
Undercutting, though, however wide,
would always need prostration. Miners eased
their bodies into fissures, on one side.
Before he was exposed, each man ensured
the place was safe, with adequate support.
His head would be provided with a board
or small three-legged stool that could be brought
beneath his thigh when crouching, holding down
the object, as the coal began to drown.

CHOCKS

The chocks obeyed like robots. Metal arms
would slowly rise or fall, responding to
a lever. They had surreal charm —
two hundred in a row, in broad clowns' shoes.
They stretched across the panzer, sheltering
machine-men. Would support the shifting roof
with timbers. Obediently they'd bring
the wood into position. Calm. Aloof.
Powered by hydraulics. Later on
the roof would fall behind to form the goaf,
exploded like a bomb. Automatons,
they stood unmoved, like fixed, unthinking oafs.
At times the roof stayed up, appeared to gell,
then, rumbling like earth's viscera, it fell.

THE VIEWER

The Viewer had a strange and saintly face.
Softened by experience, silently
it went around its district, place to place
examining the main roads, quietly
maintaining all in order. Shimmering,
a silveriness appearing in a lamp,
he drifted like a spirit, studying
his sixty different stations, checking damp
was drawn off from the levels, every dam
unleaking: that the bed-coal stood unhewed,
except around the entrance of the tram.
Everything was altered that he viewed.
One thought alone could constitute the whole
appearance, sound and fragrance of the coal.

THE FIREMAN

I can see him still, the fireman, clad in
a huge hood, damp sacking, carrying a
long pole with a candle at one end. Thin
and spiritual, moving along the
roads some hot and sultry August when
the firedamp spreads. The closeness and the heat
are gross. Occasionally he stops and then
his naked flame thrusts upwards when he meets
gas. Then he drops down on his face to miss
the blast. He fires three times a day. At four.
At noon. At seven. Others would dismiss
such methods. Behind a stable door
they'd use a copper line. A bare flame swung.
They watched, half choked with urine, steaming dung.

THE TIMEKEEPER

At its worst, the water reached three miles
beneath the mountain. It took three years
to drain the pit completely. For a while
old workings could be used. To get roads clear
the pumps worked night and day. The smell
was vile. The water was held partly back
by barometric pressure. When that fell
the men would leave the pit. Then things grew slack.
The timekeeper would long to keep his book,
to wander through the places of the pit
to take each name, and take his daily look
at colliers. He liked the game of wits.
Was subtle as the rest. So many skills
were needed for a man to blast or drill.

THE VENTILATOR

Even when no coal had been produced
the ventilation had to be maintained.
Old passages with rockfalls would be used.
Sometimes, though, great distances were gained
with bridges. He would cross an upcast shaft —
his Davy lamp extinguished by a blow —
in total darkness, feel a surging draught
around him, as he edged on, sure and slow,
across some narrow planking. On he'd edge,
feel the way before him with his feet,
or tap it with a stick. His knowledge
was profound. Each breeze that he would meet
was measured. He knew exactly how it blew,
as any anemometer would do.

OVERMEN

At a table, underneath the General
Regulations of the Coal Mines Act
of 1911, sit several
overmen. Their heads are crammed with facts
of mining. Their office is well-lit
and underground. Each dark head has its cap
and price-list for the piecework in the pit
(with various adjustments). Is a map
of heading, ripping, tramming, cutting holes,
each place with different costings, payments for
the rubbish coming down on top of coal,
the heavy dirt, or water. Is the war
of wits between the owners and the men,
of callous tricks, of ruthless acumen.

THE COLLIER

You see him? Sitting underneath one of
the 194 steel chocks that
hold the six-feet high translucent roof of F
54? The lamps upon his hat
are shining on the rippling stream of coal
that travels down the metal panzer belt
to the stage loader. The mineral rolls
to the first conveyor. The stern din pelts
his eardrums. Dust thickens. A knot of men
is stood beneath the props, and watching the
performance of the shearer as again
it stops, reverses, whines dementedly a
spinning disc of picks. They rip and eat.
Men feel the floor vibrating through their feet.

ACCIDENTS

Accidents were common in a mine.
By 1920, 32 an hour
were injured. Five hundred every day. Line
upon line of wounded. The pits devoured
their sacrifice. Blood was on the coal.
Odd fingers would be left. A stub of thumb.
One eyeball. Few colliers were left whole.
Unbroken. Scars were dark with carbon. Some
blue-black, like huge tattoos. Lungs tore to shreds.
The deeper that the pits began to sink,
the further that the tunnels sought the beds,
the more the miners died. They would drink
filth. Women would await the living dead.
Men pulled out by the arm, or by the head.

THE FIRE

The blaze was caused by a multiple steam-
driven engine. Ropes of thick steel wire
had rubbed on rusted piping. It seemed
that friction, overheating, made the fire.
In No.2. The place was built in stone —
or so the management believed. In fact
the area was coal. Gas had gone
into the workings, then exploded. Attacked
the roads with poisoned fumes. Five hundred men
were working at the time. Half of them
were killed. The rescuers brought three dozen
up, then panicked. In terror, tried to stem
the fire with the canal. The pit was drowned.
Men, horses and their trams, left underground.

SCULPTURES

Weeks after the explosion, when they reached
the pass between the intake and return
they found the doors still standing. These were breached,
and rescuers were able to discern
three colliers. Each was seated. On their knees
their tommy-boxes perched. One had meat
inside his cap. One man gripped a piece
of bread, that he was just about to eat.
The suck of air had killed them. It was strange
to find them there, untouched. There was no sign
of fire. No scorchings. Burns. No mark of change,
their features undisfigured, sharply lined
as sculpture. Unlike others killed by damp,
identified by numbers of a lamp.

CORPSES

Corpses, in the old days, it was said,
were left beside the roads until the
working-day was over. For the dead
were easily replaced. The collier
was expendable. Management
thought more about its beasts. An injured horse
would always be reported — an event
to reckon with. An asset. And of course
explosions hardly changed things. Obviously
when bodies have been charred you do not bring
them home upon a bier. Immediately
they're carted up the mountain. Men would fling
five dozen in a pit, back underground,
uncoffined, in a massive, unfenced mound.

THE LAMP

Davy had been quite specific on the
wire gauze of his lamp. Insisted that
748 holes per
sq.in. were the minimum allowed. At
the framework and the fittings any gap
was stopped. A half-shield also should be set
to keep off rapid currents of the gas.
Red-hot wire was dangerous. But colliers let
the rule-book slide. Took little notice. Holes
were far too large — the framework far too loose.
And shields were non-existent. Powdered coal
and grease stuck to the gauze. Abuse
was usual, and far too prevalent.
The lamps made risk of fire more imminent.

METHANE

As long ago as 1839
methane gas was led from collieries
in four-inch pipes. They climbed in metal lines
straight to the stocks. It burned there furiously
by day and night, stretching in the wind
great oriflammes. Ribbons were strewn out
like pennants, nine feet long. All would find
the roaring was enormous. They would shout
full blast at one another and compare
it to a furnace, for the quantity of gas
was massive. Agents watched it in still air
dance upwards like a huge leaf as they'd pass
and wondered how that violence could be used
for boilers, and its heat controlled, suffused.

WATERS

Getting to the face they often swam.
Water would collect inside the dip
at week-ends. Men would climb into the tram
and run on down the slope. The morning trip
was risky. Several times they passed beneath
thick liquid and were hauled out by their legs
half-drowned. They did not worry. Drawing breath
they laughed, shook off the black ooze and the dregs,
then fell upon the vein, impenitent.
By Monday there was water to the thigh.
Men didn't care. The coal was excellent
with plenty of wide clearance. Finally
it had to be abandoned, though in time
it drained itself. Stood empty, in its prime.

LOVERS

She did not need a reason for her love.
Things happened in completeness. All the stress
of pitwork was quite absent. Fears could move
a little, now and then. But one caress
curtailed them. She would press his yellow skin
and feel the healing wounds, the scars tattooed
by coal-dust. Lie beside his body, spin
in bliss-light. Part. Then watch the silver moods
of moonlight. See the grey rays clean the mine
like stone-dust, as the winter clouds would pass
like froth across the washeries, refine
like agitated bubbles, as each mass
would swirl up in a glowing monochrome
and separate the pit-dirt in its foam.

MAGIC

In deep mines where the temperature is high
it's naturally important to reduce
humidity. Wet heat soon stupefies
a miner. So dry air is introduced.
But then, of course, the coal-dust can explode,
and once it has been triggered it is much
more dangerous than firedamp. Down the roads
it gathers force, momentum, quick as touch.
Each morning when he'd gone off to the pit
she found she scattered water, that she'd pass
a hand in ritual movements, open it
as if she spread white stonedust which would cast
protection through his district, like a lamp
approaching subtle clouds of after-damp.

THE PIT STACK

Columns, someone said, are linking rods.
Join up earth with heaven. Their bricks allow
real commerce with the conference of gods
above us. They're holy, show us how
our life should be attached, so that the flow
of grace stays unabated. She, of course,
knew differently. Pit stack fumes would blow
into her garden, blacken blossom, force
their way in through her window, scattering
a covering of mine-dirt. They would put
a patina of filth on everything:
would get into the bedclothes, fill his suit
with soft black flakes. Premonitory fear
dyed any shape; scarce visible, but there.

SUFFERING

She knew the risks. The mines were violent.
Accidents too frequent. Understood
their woundings in her body. What each meant.
The glancing of some bone against hard wood.
A hand clasped round the steel rim of a tram
that has its fingers severed by the belt.
The runaways that happen. That could slam
straight through you, crush the flesh. She often felt
her limbs were being lacerated, bruised.
Blood-clots would be found beneath her skin.
Big blisterings. Deep scars. She felt abused,
completely unprotected in her thin
integument. Persisted. Stayed alive.
Only bled for two shifts out of five.

TARTS

Damaging the lamp-light, here they stand
in brutal self-assurance, flesh for sale,
loins greasy as an oil-box. Urgent hands
now snake out at the miscellaneous males
that tumble down the gutters. Offering
a quick transfiguration, sudden awe,
a luminous renewal, they swiftly fling
their punters in an outhouse, to a floor
heaped up with bags of cotton. Or abuse
some pit-store where they lunge and undulate
by bins of nuts and bolts, of nails and screws,
thick bars and heavy brackets. Correlate,
then finish with a harsh climactic fart
that snarls into the rafters, blasts apart.

REVENANTS

Dying was too public in the rows.
Pain was overheard. The walls too thin.
Coughs scratched the ears like sandpaper. Would grow
in violence through the night. Men would begin
to witness, feel clairvoyant, start to see
how sleepers left their bodies. Lifting, span
like thistledown on roof-tops, carelessly,
and then returned, still dreaming. Spirits ran
at random. And sometimes in the gloom
the woman who'd had cancer of the breast
groaned slowly as she walked around a room,
still staring in a terrible unrest
at moonlight, as it shone down hour by hour
its full 800,000 candlepower.

ZION CHAPEL

It was the melodies that mattered.
The Sunday hymns would gust across the mine
through the black snow. The great chords shattered
atheism. Each building seemed to shine
like ice-cased coal: electrified, would flame
like gunflash silhouettes. Eyes opened, wide-
awake. Through jammed and angled window-frames,
religion streamed: a brightness. Terrified,
the reprobate would tremble. Dark ducts leaked.
Thoughts of black damnation seared their eyes
and sprang like tears of tar across their cheeks.
Hot sweats drenched their bodies. Agonised
imaginations cried out their desires.
Their lives of double-darkness turned to fire.

THE FARRIER

Horses had their stables underground.
The farrier was the strong man in the pit.
He shod six dozen creatures. If he found
a beast had been maltreated, he would hit
its haulier to the floor, flat on his back.
Sick horses would be taken in to rest.
Men questioning his orders would be sacked.
If anything should happen to a beast
it had to be reported instantly.
He knew its tricks and habits, how it hauled.
His horses knew their districts thoroughly,
responded to their colliers when they called
each morning, at the dawn. Each knew its shift,
would wait to hear the door-bar start to lift.

BLIND HORSES

Blind horses were as useful underground
as sighted. They knew the black map of the pit
as if the roads were lighted. Colliers found
them handy when a lantern went unlit —
just gripped hold of a tail-root, then were
taken out. Occasionally a horse got
lost or panicked. Suddenly in terror
it would bolt into a wind-hole, where it shot
right to the top, and stuck there, on its side,
all four legs pinned beneath it: firmly jammed.
And others would run wild. Were pacified
by waste dipped in the black grease for the trams.
Men smeared it on a sprag, a metal bar,
then thrust it in the horse's rushing jaw.

PIT HORSES

Pit horses bite more often than they kick.
Retaliate when nipped, but bide their time,
take vengeance when it's offered. Know each trick.
Mine-wise, they remember any crime
against them. Know their way about a pit
unerringly. Hold back their haulier when
the beast in front is dangerous. They fit
deft hooves between steel rollers, stop and then
consider, set a shoe upon the floor
before they cross a railway or its rope
to see which part has passed, the tail or fore,
before they will continue. Like to grope
for clover, or for sugar. For a jest
will drag their teeth across a collier's chest.

HOLIDAYS

Holidays? Two weeks in open air
each second year. Some would refuse to go
into the cage, kicked and backed until their
haulier dragged them in. Left out in the flow
of wind-fields, abandoned to the light,
their pupils shrank to tiny specks of coal,
sheer diamond-hardened carbon. Used to night,
they staggered round, half-blinded, lost control,
ran wildly across the pastures. Finally
they'd huddle in a corner, shuddering,
suffering the cold bewilderedly,
and terrified of freedom. Shivering,
longing for the dark pit, for a load
to haul along an airway or a road.

EXPLOSIONS

At times there'd be explosions. Things would roll
a little. Glasses shook. But soon she'd shut
up consciousness. Just colliers. Miners getting coal
with gunpowder. Just shot-holes being cut
by cast-iron bars with arc-shaped chisel ends.
Men later on used mandrels. He'd explained
the way a hole was filled. His hand would send
the charge into the wall. He then would train
a needle through the centre. Then wet clay
would tamp the charge. The needle was removed.
Touchpaper then was added. Finally
the fuse would be ignited. He had loved
to tease at this point. She understood.
One then ran off as quickly as one could.

COAL TRAINS

Sometimes, in a sleepless summer night,
she'd listen to the coal-trains, hear the trucks
that clanked along the railway through the bright
grey rays of moonlight, how they struck
the gradient of the incline, rang on bends,
protesting at the overloaded freight
that sang out from the flanges. Sounds would send
odd echoes through her memory, create
an image of her father, as they'd sit
at dusk upon a bridge, in fine warm rain,
identify the coal from different pits.
It glistened like the finest cellophane,
shone dark as tar. At length they saw, with fear,
the red lamps of the guard's van disappear.

MOURNING, MORNING

There you'd see her, standing in the dawn,
a woman with a lighted cigarette
behind a window. Trying not to mourn
in the black rows. Unable to forget
bereavement. Remembering perhaps
some minor act of love that fell like light
upon the nature of existence. Scraps
of conversation, passed into the night,
distorted into complex epigrams
on someone who had filled in waiting-time
with algebra: who'd chalk upon his tram
differential equations. Not climb
through management, surveying. Keep his class
despite examinations he would pass.

NATURE

Nature kept returning. Unperturbed,
a swarm of bees would gather in the bridge
like a black womb. Seemed wholly undisturbed
by engines and the coal trucks, the language
of the pit. Red foxes crossed the tips,
would pad along the rain-diluted mud
of towpaths. The poplars in the strips
would fill with April cuckoos. Flower buds
would thrust up through the cinders and at dawn
a blackbird fluted gaily. But at dusk
the thrush began its rhetoric, forlorn
and single. Then the mountain, like a tusk,
would stab back at the moon, and once again
she'd feel his body's absence, writhe with pain.

THE COAL PICKER

By thirty she was over. Hair in strings.
All her teeth had rotted. Rain would pelt
her body, add its share of suffering
to the day's toil. The slowly moving belt
crawled onwards. She removed the larger coal
for dressing. Would strip away the slack
and other slatey matter. There the soul
died. Skin as rough as hessian, blueish black,
at times she'd stand and watch the odd designs
of wagons. Bearing fifty hundredweight
of separated coal, they moved in lines
like large inverted prisms. They would grate
each time the brake was used. Their curious space
was emptied by a trap-door at the base.

WASHERWOMEN

Over there they knelt, with women from the
copper-works, in the old days, yes, those
colliers' wives, on Mondays. There was a
sense of joining in a rite. Shirts and hose
were washed clean in the river, in the clear
cool water. They bent there, on the far bank,
on that shelving beach. A teacher would appear
to fill the sand-trays from the school, sank
slightly. They worked just below the spring.
They walked home with wet clothes upon their heads
in baskets, laughing. You'd see them crossing
the bridge, singing. But then the stream went dead
with mine-water. Where the spring boiled, one could see
a clarity in blackness, fitfully.

FIGHTING WIVES

Out there, upon the turnpike, they would fight,
the colliers' wives. Bare-breasted, in the mud,
waged wash-house wars, defended baking-rights
in the old way. Burst eyebrows. Sprayed with blood
their circling spectators. Arms like puncheons,
their legs as squat as roof-props, breathing rage
like pit-stacks, their fists would battle on
with uppercuts and swings. Some would engage
like bantams, like a pair of well-matched cocks,
their wings unclipped, legs armed with spurs of steel,
that waited several minutes, still as chocks,
and silent, till at last one bird would feel
the time right to attack, attempt to fly
and pierce its dead opponent through the eye.

PIT VILLAGE

She knew it all. The black rows. Colliers' dwellings,
solidly constructed, back to back,
sunless. The abandoned workings. Sprawling
ash-heaps. The mountain, full of gas, of black
thick veins. To right, mine-buildings. Offices.
The engine-house and tommy-shed. The rails
that sank down on the incline. Passed bosses'
separate single houses, on the trail
to the canal. Sidings. Pubs where men would lurch
on rest-days. Drink off anguish. Argue. Brawl
outside the iron-railed graveyard. Then the church.
The parson who would take a funeral
while sitting in the sexton's wheelbarrow,
too drunk to stand, too sick with vertigo.

THE RESURRECTION

For him it was a literal event.
The Resurrection of the Dead. You died,
then slept awhile. Then trumpeters were sent,
awakening. And then the crucified
returned. Old colliers would solidify
again, translucent. With their pupils dark,
they'd listen, hear which one of them would fry
in Hell. The lampless ones were for it. Clerks
that cheated. The Irish women fighting
in the street with British girls, bare-breasted.
The doctor's young assistant, bellowing
through the black rows, having just ingested
strychnine: that convulsing suicide
whose death had been prolonged, undignified.

THE FLOOD

Mining causes problems. It disturbs
the underlying strata of the earth
in unexpected places. Whole suburbs
are affected. But also it is worth
remembering that even up at height
huge reservoirs can fracture. Which is what
once happened on a normal summer night
in 1875. A stone dam that
was holding back deep water shifted, cracked.
The downpour joined the river and canal.
The water-wash was rapid. In its track
it swept away each house from the locale.
Sleepers drowned. The rescuers could see
them caught up in the branches of the trees.

SNOW

How strange it was, that snow. It was like a
burial service: something being scattered
on the open and familiar,
a white annihilation. All altered.
The bulk stuff seemed to vanish without trace —
things stored in the open, roof supports,
pit-props, rails, shaft-linings. Every place
was smothered. The vision could not sort
the joiner's from the main explosive store,
the smithy from the air-compressor house.
The aerial ropes were thickened. People saw
that everything was changing. It would rouse
anxieties, to watch the snowflakes there
appear to lift huge buildings through the air.

THE MAGIC APPLE TREE

Risen from his catacombs of coal,
the collier, grimed and blackened by the pit,
would pause behind the railings. There he'd roll
his white eyes like a minstrel. Moonlit
fruit hung in the garden, luminous
as pit-lamps, where the massive apple tree
was settling into autumn. Numinous,
it spread its boughs towards him, copiously
encumbered by its crop. Huge spheres would swell.
The faintest breeze would pick away the leaves
and pluck the fruit. The magic apples fell.
Would thud like plums. At times he'd reach to heave
a twig, a branch towards him, tear it off
like someone needing healing. Then would cough.

STRIKE

A union official sits inside
the main canteen. It's crowded. Thick with heat
and general excitement. Strikes provide
an unexpected holiday. A treat.
Since everything is out of their control
they might as well enjoy it. Wander. Roam
the backstreets. Then get drunk. Forget the coal.
Some men will bet on horses. Some go home
and seize the wife. Grow amorous. Cuddle her
and take her to a bedroom. All the men
had downed tools at the work-face. A shearer.
Broken down. The power-loader then
refused to work another. In spite of shouts
of docking pay, the whole shift had walked out.

THE DOLE QUEUE

The nature of the dole queue would depend
upon its various members. Some men wept.
Looked suicidal. Others would pretend
it simply made no difference. Others kept
a show of manly patience. None the less
each felt of course the sheer indignity
of standing in the rain, the ritual stress
of bowing down to others passively —
no more than a statistic in a book,
a figure in a ledger. It was just
the same thing for the pensioners. They took
the same type of abuse, the same mistrust.
Just turned up at the colliery, quite meek,
at times set by the offices each week.

COAL PICKERS

The strikers soon grew desperate for coal.
He looked out from the window to the tips.
The thieving was colossal. Up there whole
black households of the colliers fought to strip
the last slack from the rubbish of the roads,
the rock cut from a roof-arch. Here and there,
occasionally pitched battles would explode
between the miners. Stones flew through the air
that smouldered down the valley. On the dumps
the women knelt with children as their eyes
would rummage through the dust, pounce on some lump
and wipe it clean, minutely scrutinize,
then set it in some meagre sack of fuel
as if it were a diamond or a jewel.

THE ENGINE MAN'S DREAM

At times his arm would lift out of his dream.
It glimmered in the moonbeams, slag-scarred, bent,
and wrestled with the waters. Wreathed in steam,
it fought the dirts, the scaly excrements,
struggled as the thick precipitate
was hardened to a sediment, a crust,
hard-firing, till the metal of the plate
could not absorb the heat's excited lust.
The boiler tube was dropping. Men took flight.
Illumined by the red glare of the fires
they rushed away stark naked through the night,
blundered through the hot ash and the mires
to lift with the explosion, in the spate
of scalding slimes and fitments, scattered slate.

THE DRIVER

Nothing's now forbidden or taboo.
No figure claims the centre of this space,
emerges as a driver, one who knew
the nature of the ironwork in the place,
the strength of each resistance. How to set
the pressure of the steam, its pace and strength
before it reached the piston through the jet
to send it through the cylinder's full length.
Controlled the risk of drop, the sudden jerk
that draws upon the stock too violently
with seething ebullitions, a berserk
inruption of the muds as suddenly
they boil with salts and oxides and become
churned up with surface scurf, and foam, and scum.

MARS

Old clouds hang like mine-gas, heavy damp.
You watch the planet rising through the night.
Suspended like some dull sepulchral lamp
the low glow of its sacrificial light
burns slowly on the dumps, a crimson red.
It mingles, stains the shaft-smoke, dirty steam.
A memory of the lost uncoffined dead
it rises to a brighter, fuller gleam,
aggressive, like some fierce antagonist,
the red pit of a socket in a face,
the eye blown from its fastenings. Through the mist
it palpitates in blackness, filling space,
a fire-prayer for reprisals, hot and raw,
and scorching like the origin of war.

SILICOSIS

The dust had got him. Filled his lungs with grit.
He sat up nights, coughing like a pick
at the soft coal. Each wheeze a wound. The pit
still gassed him, and the mucus bubbled, thick
as a black stew. Clouds hung like punctured lungs
on the dark tips. But sometimes, in the day,
he'd sit out in his pit-clothes, watch the tongues
of smoke lick from the stack. At times he'd say
the hill had turned transparent. He could see
the far end of the mine, the curving roads
that bent beneath the mountain, every
dead horse, and boy and collier. Or explode
with sudden gusts of dread. In night attire
would shout into the street, "The pit's on fire!"

IN THE WATER

Corpses in the water won't lie quiet.
People see them floating in the deep,
drifting in an amniotic night
all angles. Re-enacting in their sleep
that moment when the burning in the coal
was drenched by a diversion, a canal
that flushed into the pit and drowned the whole
length of the workings. It was all
too desperate, that panic. Men could see
the river quickly lifting in the shaft.
The manager took flight immediately.
The miners would have killed him. Then have laughed:
weighted him to lie there with the rest
beneath the mountain's tumulus, unblessed.

THE SURVIVOR

It did not make him happy. He never
laughed in celebration of the fact
that he alone remained. A survivor.
Others had been broken, gassed. He, intact,
just drifted round the village, stopping now
like paper, then proceeding, carried round
and pondering on providence, on how
deep guilt could be released. At times he found
he willed some sudden failure of the beam
at the steam stroke, cracked it at the gudgeon,
split in two. Then moved into a dream
of shaft-collapse, the demolition
of an engine, experiencing as he'd pass
some ninety tons of iron and tarnished brass.

GHOSTS

Any third-rate medium would do:
could pick them up, the roving, earth-bound ones
who finished in the pit, the colliers who
were caught out by a roof-fall, sudden runs
that pinned them down with timbers. One can sense
their presence by the shaft, the rising cage,
tugging with their usual insolence
at night-shifts, shouting out in sudden rage
to find that they're ignored, just brushed aside
with innocent indifference. All are here —
those broken by explosions, those who died
from runaways, were fixed in sudden fear
to find things overwinding: with a shock
were shot across the headgear from the stocks.

THE DERELICT ENGINE HOUSE

Its acid irrigation of the land
is over. Muds no longer burn your feet.
No smoke is stretched in laminated bands
like coal-seams. Old winds enter, winter sleet.
Its cylinder is smashed, its cast-iron heart.
No measurer's delivering the coals:
no figures in the columns of a chart
recording every bushel of the fuel.
A sheep shakes with a dry asthmatic cough.
It scratches through the black screes of the dumps.
There is no counting of the number of
the strokes made in a month. No grinding pumps.
No engine-man to punish or correct.
No penalty imposed for this neglect.

CLOSURE

Now it is the silence that unnerves.
The static trigonometry of wires.
Stiff pulley-wheels, unmoving. Rusted curves
of pit-track. No living steam. No fires.
The cages on their catches. Washeries
go first, then screening-plant. Pumping-engines
stay. Their houses loom like mysteries,
half-drowned in briars and ivy. Most machines
dismantle. Yes, a stack will stay erect.
Fans and headstocks sometimes will survive.
The dirt-tips, though, will linger, derelict,
on mountains. Grow more liquid, start to give,
a tide of vulgar slurry, carbon silt
advancing with the gravity of guilt.

HISTORY

A coal-mine, say two hundred years ago,
would not show many details. There would be
an atmospheric engine, boilers, two
short shafts, with pulleys and a chimney
and a small hut. Three top-men might be found,
one holding a small horse. Few signs of slack –
screening was effected underground,
the small coal raked away and sent straight back.
Little waste remained. The stall-man gobbed
the dirt. It was considered an offence
to send it from the mine. The coal was robbed
then left. There was no negligence.
No filth was piled in mountains, strewn about –
just soil wound out in sinking, heading out.